CAT Files

I0880446

Cheetah

WRITTEN BY
BETHANY LATHAM

KidHaven
PUBLISHING

Published in 2027 by
KidHaven Publishing, an Imprint of Greenhaven Publishing, LLC
2544 Clinton St., Buffalo, NY 14224

© 2025 BookLife Publishing Ltd.

Written by: Bethany Latham
Edited by: Rebecca Phillips-Bartlett
Designed by: Ker Ker Lee

All facts, statistics, web addresses, and URLs in this book were verified as valid and accurate at time of writing. No responsibility for any changes to external websites or references can be accepted by either the author or publisher.

Cataloging-in-Publication Data
Names: Latham, Bethany.
Title: Cheetah / Bethany Latham.
Description: Buffalo, NY : KidHaven Publishing, 2027. | Series: Cat files | Includes glossary and index.
Identifiers: ISBN 9781534569560 (pbk.) | ISBN 9781534569577 (library bound) | ISBN 9781534569584 (ebook)
Subjects: LCSH: Cheetah--Juvenile literature. | Cheetah--Behavior--Juvenile literature. | Endangered species--Africa--Juvenile literature.
Classification: LCC QL737.C23 L384 2027 | DDC 599.759--dc23

All rights reserved.
No part of this book may be reproduced in any form without permission in writing from the publisher, except by a reviewer.

Printed in China

CPSIA compliance information: Batch #QS27KH: For further information contact Greenhaven Publishing LLC at 1-844-317-7404.

Please visit our website, www.greenhavenpublishing.com.
For a free color catalog of all our high-quality books, call toll free 1-844-317-7404 or fax 1-844-317-7405.

Find us on

Photo Credits – Images courtesy of Shutterstock.com, unless otherwise stated.

Cover & Recurring – Stu Porter, Wayne Marinovich, fototrips, Jemastock, graficriver_icons_logo, Vector Tradition. 2–3 – Sumaira35. 4–5 – Michal Ninger, Natureyz Lenz, Holly S Cannon, Milan Zygmunt. 6–7 – JonathanC Photography, Nick Dale Photo. 8–9 – Nastya Smirnova RF, muratart. 10–11 – Eric Isselee, Phillip van Zyl. 12–13 – seeshooteatrepeat, Benny Marty, Abhishek Raviya, Shlomi Hazan. 14–15 – Nick Dale Photo, Arturo de Frias, Martin Mecnarowski. 16–17 – Nick Dale Photo, Ahmed Abubasel. 18–19 – alvarog1970, Gunter Nuyts. 20–21 – Chaithanya Krishnan, Henk Bogaard. 22–23 – Wayne Marinovich, Henk Bogaard.

Contents

Words that look like this can be found in the glossary on page 24.

Big Cats

Big cats are a group of carnivorous mammals. Carnivores eat meat. Mammals are warm-blooded and have a backbone. Scientists group big cats together because they have a lot in common, including their rough tongues.

Tiger

Lion

Cheetahs look like big cats. However, scientists do not group these animals with big cats, such as lions, tigers, and leopards. Cheetahs belong to different animal group, called Felinae.

Snow leopard

Cheetah

FACT FILE

DIET:	Carnivore
ANIMAL TYPE:	Mammal
HUNTING:	Predator

Cheetahs

Most cheetahs live in Africa. They are mostly found in Kenya, Tanzania, Namibia, and Botswana. A small number of cheetahs also live in an Asian country called Iran. Cheetahs are the world's fastest land mammal.

Cheetahs can run up to around 71 miles (114 km) an hour.

FACT FILE

CONTINENT:	Africa and Asia
SIZE:	Around 39 to 59 inches (100 to 150 cm) long (without tail)
WEIGHT:	Usually between 77 and 143 pounds (35 and 65 kg)
SPEED:	Up to 71 miles (114 km) an hour

Cheetahs cannot roar. They chirp and purr instead.

Habitat

An animal's natural home is called its habitat. A habitat gives an animal everything it needs to survive, including food, water, and shelter. Cheetahs can live in many different habitats, including mountains and deserts.

Most cheetahs live on grasslands called savannas. Savannas are flat and open, so the cheetahs have plenty of space. Savannas are always warm. They have two seasons—a dry season and a wet season.

The dry season is usually longer than the wet season.

Body

Cheetahs all have some important body parts:

Cheetahs' bodies are thin and agile.

Cheetahs have long tails. They help cheetahs balance while running.

Cheetahs' legs are long and powerful to help them run.

Cheetahs have spotted fur with black markings on their faces.

Cheetahs have short teeth.

Unlike big cats, cheetahs' claws are not fully retractable. Their claws grip the ground when they run.

Blending In

The spots on a cheetah's fur help it camouflage itself. The black spots and golden fur look like shadows in the golden savanna grass. They make the cheetah's body harder to see.

FACT FILE

COLOR:	Light brown to golden, with some black and white
PATTERN:	Solid spots
FUR LENGTH:	Short
CAMOUFLAGE TYPE:	Concealing and fixed

This is known as concealing camouflage. It is also fixed camouflage because the fur does not change color. Each cheetah has unique spots.

Hunting Prey

Cheetahs eat small to medium-sized animals, such as gazelles and impalas. Cheetahs hunt during the day. Cheetahs use their powerful eyesight to spot their prey. They climb termite hills to see farther.

Termite hill

Impala

Gazelle

The black marks under a cheetah's eyes act like sunglasses.

Cheetahs chase their prey to catch it. The chase usually only lasts around 20 seconds because cheetahs get tired quickly.

FACT FILE

TAIL LENGTH: 24 to 33 inches (60 to 85 cm)

STRIDE LENGTH: Around 23 feet (7 m)

FOOD EATEN: Around 7 pounds (3 kg) a day

Family Life

Female cheetahs are solitary. This means they live alone, unless they are raising young. Female cheetahs have large territories and travel around a lot. They usually follow their prey as it moves.

Male cheetahs live in small groups called coalitions. Coalitions usually include two to four brothers. The brothers are very close. Cheetahs often stay in these groups for their whole lives.

FACT FILE

GROUP NAME:	Coalition
GROUP SIZE:	Usually two to four
COMMUNICATION:	Chirping

Raising Young

Young cheetahs are called cubs. The mother is usually pregnant for around three months. She then usually has three to five cubs at once. Some cheetahs have as many as eight cubs at once.

FACT FILE

NAME:	Cub
NUMBER:	Usually three to five
PREGNANCY LENGTH:	Around three months
WHEN FULLY GROWN:	Two years

The mother raises her cubs on her own. The cubs stay with their mother for around 18 months. They are fully grown after two years.

Cats in Danger

Scientists label cheetahs as vulnerable. This means their numbers are falling in the wild. Cheetahs need lots of space to live in. Human activity, such as farming, leaves cheetahs with less land to hunt on.

Some farmers kill cheetahs to protect their animals. Some groups are giving farmers guard animals, such as dogs, to help scare cheetahs away. This means the farmers are less likely to kill the cheetahs.

Some people kill cheetahs to sell their body parts.

Cat Files

Cheetahs are amazing cats. They are perfectly built for speed and blending into their grassy habitats. Would you like to see a cheetah in the wild?

Roar-Some Roundup

CONTINENT:	Africa and Asia
HABITAT:	Grasslands, mountains, deserts
FUR LENGTH:	Short
SPEED:	Up to 71 miles (114 km) an hour
STRIDE LENGTH:	Around 23 feet (7 m)

Wild cats are important animals. How could you help cheetahs? You can do some research with a grown-up!

Glossary

agile able to move quickly and easily

camouflage to hide by blending into the surroundings

predator an animal that hunts other animals for food

pregnant when a female animal has one or more babies growing inside her

prey animals that are hunted by other animals for food

retractable able to be pulled back or in, such as claws

stride length the distance between two steps of the same foot

territories areas claimed and defended by an animal

unique one of a kind

Index